CANDICE BAILEY   PROPERLYPROSPERREALTY.COM   @PROPERLYPROSPERREALTY

Paths

Unauthorized Occupants

A STEP-BY-STEP GUIDE
Navigating through issue of Unauthorized Occupants.
A Guide for Homeowners and Property Managers

The Author

Candice Monique Bailey: Navigating Success in Real Estate

Candice Monique Bailey is an esteemed professional in the realm of property management and real estate. Her journey in the industry began as a leasing agent, a role that sparked her passion for the world of real estate. Over the years, she advanced through the ranks, from being an assistant property manager to a property administrator, demonstrating an unwavering commitment to her field.

With her Salesperson and property manager licenses in hand, Candice took the leap to become a Broker Salesperson. This marked a pivotal point in her career. Her drive and determination led her to achieve the esteemed position of Managing Broker of Property Manager and PM Licenses at Properly Prosper Realty.

Candice's motivation to share her knowledge and experiences through these real estate and property management guides is rooted in her desire to make the industry more accessible and comprehensible for newcomers and industry veterans alike. She believes in empowering individuals to navigate the intricacies of property management and real estate with confidence, and these guides are a testament to her dedication.

Candice's remarkable journey in the industry, from humble beginnings to a position of leadership, serves as an inspiring example for those looking to prosper in the world of real estate. Through her words and insights, she aims to provide guidance, knowledge, and encouragement to readers on their own paths to success.

MORE ON PROPERLYPROSPERREALTY.COM

Statement on the Importance of the Guide:

INTRO:

If you're a homeowner or a property manager facing the challenge of an unauthorized occupant, you're not alone. This common issue in property management is particularly relevant in Las Vegas, Nevada, where licensed property managers are empowered to handle the legal aspects of property management, as sanctioned by the state. However, for many individuals, the intricacies of this process may remain unfamiliar territory. In this guide, my aim is to bridge that knowledge gap.

Throughout the following pages, a real-life situation I personally encountered will serve as a practical example. You'll also find a systematic breakdown of the steps required to effectively resolve issues related to unauthorized occupants, whether you're a homeowner or a property manager. In addition to these insights, we'll provide you with essential resources for escalating problems to a legal dispute, offer email templates for streamlined communication, and present a detailed step-by-step correspondence guide. This guide is tailored to empower both homeowners and property managers, offering valuable insights into the intricacies of unauthorized occupants in the realm of property management.

We are committed to equipping licensed professionals with the knowledge and resources they need to excel in the real estate and property management industry. Simultaneously, we empower property owners, residents, and the public with valuable insights to protect property rights and ensure a transparent, accountable, and harmonious housing environment.

Our mission is to bridge the gap between professionals and the community, fostering an environment where ethical practices and residents' well-being are paramount. As unauthorized occupants continue to be a concern in the real estate industry, our resources are critical tools to create a harmonious and mutually beneficial environment for all residents and property stakeholders, ultimately ensuring the integrity of the housing industry.

Statement on the Importance of the Guide:

EMPOWERING THE REAL ESTATE COMMUNITY

Our series of real estate and property management guides, including "Unauthorized Occupants: A Guide for Rental Property Owners and Managers," holds immense significance for both licensed professionals, the general public, and residents in the housing industry. Education in this field is essential to promote ethical practices, safeguard property rights, and ensure fair treatment for all involved.

We are committed to equipping licensed professionals with the knowledge and resources they need to excel in the real estate and property management industry. Simultaneously, we empower property owners, residents, and the public with valuable insights to protect property rights and ensure a transparent, accountable, and harmonious housing environment.

Our mission is to bridge the gap between professionals and the community, fostering an environment where ethical practices and residents' well-being are paramount. As unauthorized occupants continue to be a concern in the real estate industry, our resources are critical tools to create a harmonious and mutually beneficial environment for all residents and property stakeholders, ultimately ensuring the integrity of the housing industry.

Statement on the Importance of the Guide:

DISCLAIMER:

The content presented in this book, titled "Navigating Unauthorized Occupants: A Guide for Homeowners and Property Managers," is provided for informational purposes only. The information contained herein is based on general knowledge and industry practices up to the knowledge cutoff date in November 2023.

The book aims to offer insights, recommendations, and strategies related to the prevention and management of unauthorized occupants in a property management context. However, it is important to note that laws, regulations, and best practices in the field of property management may vary across regions and are subject to change.

Readers are advised to seek professional advice and consult with legal experts, property management professionals, or relevant authorities in their specific jurisdiction to address their unique circumstances. The author and publisher disclaim any liability for actions taken by readers based on the information provided in this book.

The content does not constitute legal advice or a substitute for professional consultation. It is recommended that readers verify information with current legal authorities and tailor strategies to suit their specific situations. The author and publisher are not responsible for any consequences arising from the use or interpretation of the information presented in this book.

Readers are encouraged to stay informed about local laws and regulations, seek legal counsel when necessary, and adapt the principles and recommendations in this book to align with their individual circumstances.

CHAPTER N.1

Chapter 1: The Prevalence of Unauthorized Occupants

· The prevalence of unauthorized occupants
· Legal aspects in property management
· Purpose of the guide

Chapter 1: The Prevalence of Unauthorized Occupants

THE UNINVITED GUESTS

In the intricate world of property management, unauthorized occupants, colloquially known as squatters, have become a recurring challenge. These uninvited guests operate in a legal gray area, occupying vacant or underutilized properties without the owner's permission, casting a shadow over property ownership and management.

PROPERTY OWNERS UNDER SIEGE

This issue has become a thorn in the side of property owners. They grapple with the daunting task of dealing with these unwelcome occupants. Eviction processes can be labyrinthine, properties can suffer damage, and owners may find themselves embroiled in legal disputes, putting the sanctuary of their investments at risk.

PROPERTY MANAGERS ON THE FRONT LINES

Property managers, as the guardians of these properties, find themselves at the forefront of the battle against unauthorized occupants. They are tasked with staying abreast of the ever-evolving legal landscape and devising effective strategies to protect properties on behalf of their clients – the property owners. It's a relentless responsibility that demands both vigilance and expertise

Chapter 1: The Prevalence of Unauthorized Occupants

NAVIGATING THE LEGAL MAZE

IThe legal aspects surrounding unauthorized occupants are intricate and vary significantly by location. Property managers and owners must navigate local laws, eviction procedures, and property rights. The introduction of eviction moratoriums during the COVID-19 pandemic added new layers of complexity, with legal constraints on eviction proceedings.

THE SHADOWS OF SCAMS AND FRAUD

In the digital age, scams and fraud have found fertile ground within the property rental market. Individuals pose as property managers or owners, luring unsuspecting renters with fictitious listings and collecting payments for properties they don't have the right to rent. This epidemic of deception leads to significant financial losses and ensuing legal disputes.

HOMELESSNESS AND SQUATTING: A COMPLEX LINK

Homelessness, a pressing societal issue, is inextricably intertwined with unauthorized occupancy. Homeless individuals often resort to squatting in vacant properties in a desperate search for shelter. This presents a conundrum that transcends mere property management, delving into the realms of social and humanitarian concern.

Chapter 1: The Prevalence of Unauthorized Occupants

CHALLENGES IN THE RENTAL MARKET

The legal aspects surrounding unauthorized occupants are intricate and vary significantly by location. Property managers and owners must navigate local laws, eviction procedures, and property rights. The introduction of eviction moratoriums during the COVID-19 pandemic added new layers of complexity, with legal constraints on eviction proceedings.

The prevalence of unauthorized occupants has eroded trust within the rental market. Prospective renters, wary of falling victim to scams or facing unauthorized occupants, approach their housing searches with caution. The very essence of the rental market is called into question, casting a shadow over legitimate property transactions.
Reform and Regulation

In response to these challenges, some regions are considering or implementing legal reforms to address the issue of unauthorized occupants and rental scams. Property managers and owners must be vigilant about staying informed regarding these changes, both to ensure compliance and protect their vested interests.

Chapter 1: The Prevalence of Unauthorized Occupants

KNOWLEDGE: THE BEST DEFENSE

lAmidst these intricate challenges, one undeniable truth emerges – knowledge is the most potent weapon in the arsenal against unauthorized occupants and rental scams. Awareness and education are the keys to empowering property owners, managers, and renters in their quest for secure and fair property transactions. This chapter reveals the intricate challenges within the property management landscape, from unauthorized occupants and rental scams to the intertwined issue of homelessness. It underscores the importance of reform, awareness, and proactive property management practices in addressing these complex matters.

Chapter 1a: Legal Aspects in Property Management:

NAVIGATING THE LEGAL LANDSCAPE

In the realm of property management, understanding the legal aspects is akin to wielding a compass through uncharted territory. It is a terrain marked by property owners, property managers, unauthorized occupants, and the vulnerable homeless, all impacted by the intricacies of the law.

PROPERTY OWNERS' RIGHTS AND RESPONSIBILITIES

Property owners, the custodians of real estate investments, must tread cautiously within the legal framework. They bear the responsibility of safeguarding their property rights while complying with the laws governing property management. Understanding the nuances of leases, tenancy agreements, and eviction procedures is crucial to protect their assets.

PROPERTY OWNERS' RIGHTS AND RESPONSIBILITIES

Property owners, the custodians of real estate investments, must tread cautiously within the legal framework. They bear the responsibility of safeguarding their property rights while complying with the laws governing property management. Understanding the nuances of leases, tenancy agreements, and eviction procedures is crucial to protect their assets.

PROPERTY MANAGERS' LEGAL AUTHORITY

Property managers, entrusted with the management of these properties, are granted legal authority to act on behalf of property owners. However, their actions must align with the law, navigating rental agreements, eviction processes, and tenant rights. A misstep could lead to legal repercussions, making legal competence an essential trait for effective property management.

Chapter 1a: Legal Aspects in Property Management:

EVICTION AND COURT PROCEDURES

The eviction process is a legal minefield, and property managers and owners must navigate it with precision. Understanding the proper grounds for eviction, adhering to notice requirements, and following court procedures is essential. Eviction moratoriums, introduced during the COVID-19 pandemic, have further complicated this terrain, requiring compliance with ever-changing legal constraints.

HOMELESSNESS AND PROPERTY RIGHTS

The intertwining of homelessness with unauthorized occupancy raises complex ethical and legal dilemmas. Property owners often find themselves torn between asserting their property rights and recognizing the desperate need for shelter faced by homeless individuals. Legal responsibilities and moral considerations are at odds, highlighting the need for comprehensive policy solutions.

LEGAL SAFEGUARDS AGAINST SCAMS

In a world rife with scams and fraud, both property owners and renters require legal safeguards. Laws pertaining to fraudulent listings, deceptive practices, and financial scams play a pivotal role in preventing unsuspecting individuals from falling prey to property-related fraud. Legal recourse is essential for those who find themselves victims of these deceptive schemes.

REFORMS AND REGULATIONS

Recognizing the evolving challenges posed by unauthorized occupants and rental scams, some regions are considering or implementing legal reforms. These reforms aim to streamline eviction procedures, protect property owners' rights, and ensure that homeless individuals receive appropriate assistance. Property managers and owners must stay informed about these reforms to adapt and comply with the changing legal landscape.

Chapter 1a: Legal Aspects in Property Management:

SEEKING LEGAL RESOLUTION

When all else fails, the legal system remains the ultimate recourse for property owners and managers facing unauthorized occupants, scams, or related disputes. Understanding the processes for seeking legal resolution, engaging in mediation or arbitration, or pursuing litigation becomes imperative in protecting property interests.

CONCLUSION: THE LEGAL COMPASS

As we delve into the legal aspects of property management, we uncover a multifaceted terrain where property rights, legal responsibilities, and the plight of the homeless intersect. It is a landscape where the legal compass guides property owners, managers, and renters in their quest for fair and just property transactions, and where reforms strive to create a harmonious balance between rights and humanity. In the following chapters, we continue to explore the ways to navigate this complex terrain.

CHAPTER N.2

Chapter 2 : Understanding Unauthorized Occupants:

- ·Defining unauthorized occupants
- ·Common scenarios and challenges
- The legal implications

Chapter 2 : Understanding Unauthorized Occupants:

Understanding Unauthorized Occupants:

In the complex landscape of property ownership and occupancy, a group of individuals often referred to as unauthorized occupants exists. These individuals include squatters, the homeless, and those who have been duped into believing they have a legitimate right to occupy a property through various online solicitations. This chapter delves into the intricacies of this issue, shedding light on the challenges and legal considerations surrounding these unauthorized occupants.

2. - Defining unauthorized occupants:

2.1 Squatters:

The Uninvited Guests: Squatters are individuals who occupy a property without legal authorization. While the term "squatter" may conjure images of people taking over abandoned buildings, the reality is more nuanced. Squatting can occur in various types of properties, including vacant homes, abandoned commercial spaces, or even unoccupied vacation homes. Squatters often assert rights based on the principle of adverse possession, claiming that if they occupy a property for a certain period of time, they gain legal ownership.

2.2 HOMELESSNESS AND PROPERTY OCCUPANCY:

Homelessness and Property Occupancy: The issue of homelessness is a societal challenge, and the homeless population sometimes resorts to occupying vacant properties as a means of survival. Property owners must confront the delicate balance between protecting their property rights and addressing the humanitarian concerns associated with homelessness. Local governments often establish procedures for handling homelessness and may require property owners to follow specific protocols before eviction.

2.3 Online Scams and Unauthorized Occupancy:

Online Scams and Unauthorized Occupancy: In the age of the internet, scams have taken on new dimensions, including fraudulent solicitations for property occupancy. Unscrupulous individuals may pose as property owners or agents and lure unsuspecting individuals into paying rent or occupying properties they have no legal right to. Victims of online scams often find themselves facing eviction and legal challenges, even though they believed they were acting in good faith.

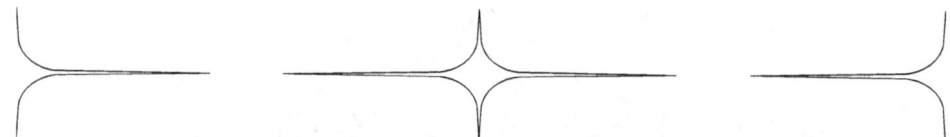

2.4 LEGAL CONSIDERATIONS AND REMEDIES:

Addressing unauthorized occupants, regardless of their category, requires an understanding of the legal framework in place. Property owners must adhere to local and state laws and, when necessary, seek legal counsel to regain possession of their properties. Eviction procedures, which vary by jurisdiction, are typically the legal means to remove unauthorized occupants. Additionally, property owners should consider preventative measures such as property security, regular inspections, and clear lease agreements to mitigate the risk of unauthorized occupancy.

2.5 CONCLUSION:

Unauthorized occupants present a complex and multifaceted challenge for property owners, communities, and policymakers. Whether they are squatters, the homeless, or victims of online scams, addressing this issue requires a delicate balancing act of legal rights, social responsibility, and compassion. In the chapters to come, we will explore the strategies and resources available to property owners dealing with unauthorized occupants and the evolving landscape of property occupancy in the digital age.

2a - Common Scenarios and Challenges:

In the world of unauthorized occupants, property owners and communities frequently encounter several common scenarios and challenges. This chapter explores these scenarios in greater detail, with a focus on squatters, the homeless, and individuals who have fallen victim to online scams, delving into the complexities and difficulties associated with each.

2a.1 Squatters:

The Tenacious Occupants: Squatters come in various forms, but the common denominator is their presence on a property without legal authorization. They often exploit loopholes or misconceptions about adverse possession laws, which grant property rights to individuals who occupy a property for a specific duration.

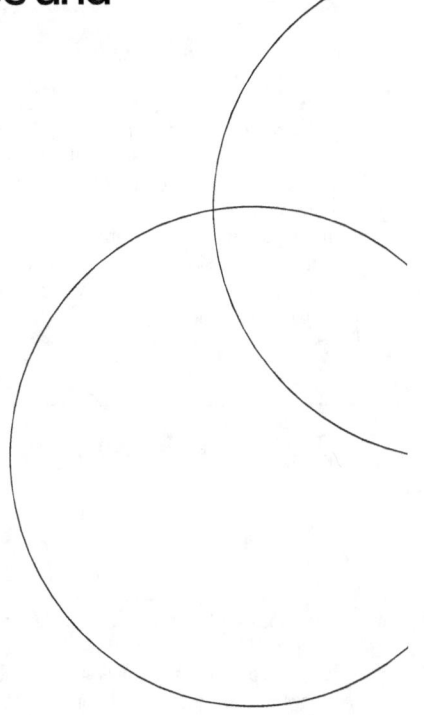

COMMON SCENARIOS INCLUDE VACANT HOMES, WHERE SQUATTERS FREQUENTLY TARGET ABANDONED OR FORECLOSED PROPERTIES, TAKING ADVANTAGE OF HOMEOWNERS' ABSENCE.

HERE'S HOW IT WORKS

In many cases, these individuals may set up makeshift living arrangements, making it difficult for property owners to regain control. Challenges with squatters include proving ownership and pursuing eviction, which can be a lengthy and costly process.

2a.2 Homelessness:

: A Complex Challenge: The issue of homelessness intersects with unauthorized occupancy, as individuals experiencing homelessness may seek shelter in vacant properties. Common scenarios include abandoned buildings, where homeless individuals often seek shelter, posing safety concerns for both the occupants and property owners. Challenges with homelessness include balancing property rights with humanitarian concerns and evicting homeless occupants, which requires a sensitive approach and coordination with local agencies.

2a.3 Online Scams:

Trapped by Deception: In the digital age, online scams have given rise to a new form of unauthorized occupancy. Individuals fall prey to fraudulent solicitations, leading to them mistakenly believing they have a legal right to occupy a property. Common scenarios include false rental listings and misleading lease agreements. Challenges with online scams include victims being caught in a legal and emotional quagmire, and property owners facing challenges in evicting these individuals.

2a.4 Finding Balance and Solutions:

Addressing common scenarios and challenges related to unauthorized occupants is a multifaceted endeavor. Property owners, communities, and local authorities must work together to strike a balance between property rights and social responsibility.

Legal Framework

Legal Framework: Understanding and navigating local and state laws regarding eviction and property rights is crucial for property owners dealing with unauthorized occupants. Preventative Measures: Property owners can take proactive measures to secure their properties, such as regular inspections, improved security, and clear lease agreements. Community Engagement: Addressing homelessness and unauthorized occupancy requires the engagement of local authorities, social services, and advocacy groups to find long-term solutions.

AS WE DELVE DEEPER

As we delve deeper into this complex issue, subsequent chapters will explore practical solutions, resources, and the evolving landscape of property occupancy in the face of these challenges.

2b.1 Squatters: The Legal Gray Area:

The presence of squatters often raises questions about property rights, adverse possession, and the eviction process. Property owners may encounter legal hurdles when attempting to remove squatters from their properties. Key legal implications include adverse possession, eviction process, and property damage caused by squatters.

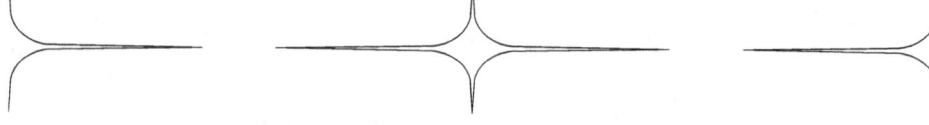

2b.2 Homelessness and Legal Obligations:

Dealing with homelessness and unauthorized occupancy on properties demands a balance between property rights and legal obligations towards homeless individuals. Legal implications related to homelessness include anti-homeless laws, due process, and human rights considerations.

2B.3 ONLINE SCAMS AND LEGAL REMEDIES:

When individuals fall victim to online scams that deceive them into occupying a property, the legal implications are primarily focused on issues of fraud and misrepresentation. Key legal considerations in such cases include fraudulent misrepresentation, lease agreements, and criminal investigations.

2b.4 Legal Strategies and Resources:

Addressing the legal implications of unauthorized occupancy requires a thorough understanding of local laws, careful documentation, and access to legal resources. Property owners, local authorities, and the occupants themselves can consider the following legal strategies and resources:

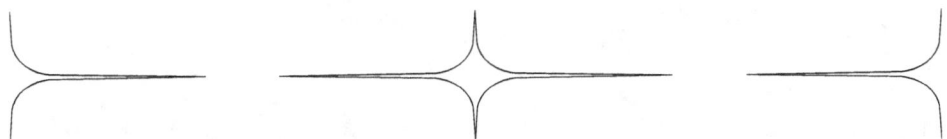

LEGAL COUNSEL:

Property owners should consult with attorneys who specialize in real estate and property law to navigate the legal process of eviction or resolving disputes. Local Laws and Regulations: Familiarize yourself with local laws and regulations that pertain to unauthorized occupancy. These laws can differ significantly depending on your jurisdiction. Alternative Dispute Resolution: In some cases, alternative dispute resolution methods, such as mediation or arbitration, may provide a more efficient way to resolve conflicts. Human Rights Organizations: Homeless individuals and their advocates can reach out to human rights organizations to ensure their rights are protected.
As we delve deeper into this complex issue, subsequent chapters will explore practical legal strategies, resources, and the evolving legal landscape of property occupancy in the context of unauthorized occupants.

2b: Legal Implications of Unauthorized Occupancy

2b: Legal Implications of Unauthorized Occupancy delves into the intricate legal aspects of dealing with unauthorized occupants. It covers the legal gray areas of squatters, the legal obligations related to homelessness, and the legal remedies available to those who have been scammed online. The chapter highlights the importance of understanding local laws, seeking legal counsel, and accessing resources to navigate the complexities of unauthorized occupancy.

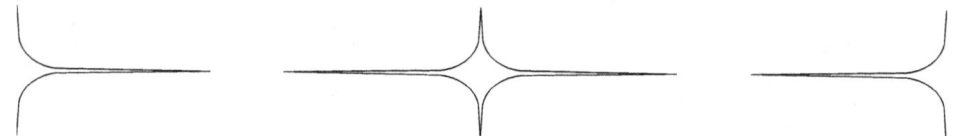

CONCLUSION:

Common Scenarios and Challenges explores the typical situations involving squatters, the homeless, and victims of online scams who believe they have the right to occupy a property. It outlines the challenges and complexities that property owners and communities face in addressing these scenarios.

n the upcoming chapters, we will provide guidance on practical solutions, resources, and evolving strategies to address this challenging issue.

CHAPTER N.3

Chapter 3: Real-Life Example

· Personal experience as a case study
· Lessons learned.

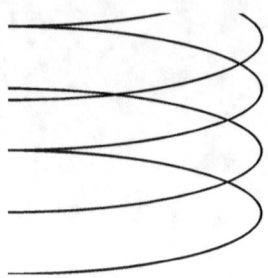

INTRODUCTION CHAPTER 3: REAL-LIFE EXAMPLE

Chapter 3: Real-Life Example

3. Lessons Learned: Insights for All

Through this deeply personal case study, we will extract invaluable lessons and insights. The experiences of Author will offer guidance and wisdom that can serve as a source of knowledge for property owners, communities, and individuals who may find themselves confronting unauthorized occupants in the future.

These lessons may encompass:
- The critical importance of routine property inspections and robust security measures in averting unauthorized occupancy.
- The significance of understanding and adhering to local laws and regulations related to eviction and property rights.
- The necessity of seeking legal counsel and navigating the intricacies of due process when faced with unauthorized occupants.
- The role of community engagement, cooperation with local authorities, and advocacy in managing and ultimately resolving such challenging situations.
- The invaluable awareness of the emotional toll and the need for support networks during the arduous journey of dealing with unauthorized occupants.

As we embark on this journey alongside Author this chapter will serve as a living testament to the tangible struggles and triumphs experienced when grappling with unauthorized occupancy. The profound lessons learned will lay the foundation for the forthcoming chapters, which will delve into practical solutions, resources, and evolving strategies to address this multifaceted issue.

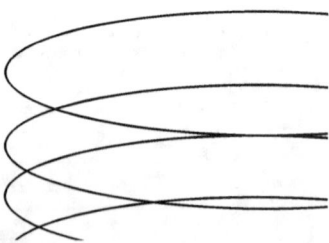

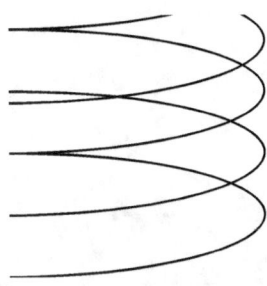

CHAPTER 3: A PERSONAL EXPERIENCE AS A CASE STUDY

In my years of working in property management, I've encountered several instances where unauthorized occupants became a significant issue. These situations can arise due to various factors we've discussed earlier, ranging from squatters to individuals who have fallen victim to rental scams. Handling these matters in property management requires a specific approach before considering escalation. It's essential to not only cross your t's and dot your i's but also to reflect on your actions and decisions.

In this chapter, I will share three scenarios from my personal experience to illustrate the challenges and solutions in managing unauthorized occupants.

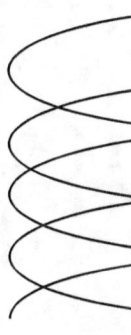

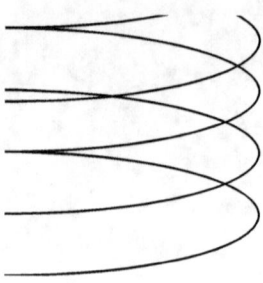

SCENARIO 1: A FRAUDULENT LEASE

One Monday, our customer service team alerted me to a resident's complaint regarding access to amenities in a property managed by a community association. The resident claimed they had been given keys to the gym and various access points, but the keys weren't working. Strangely, their information did not appear in our records as residents. As the property administrator at the time, I immediately verified our system to confirm their status, which indeed showed them as non-residents. Preparing for a difficult conversation, I contacted the unauthorized occupant. It turned out to be a family of four – two adults and two children under the age of five – who had fully furnished each room in the home. They had moved in under a fraudulent lease.

The occupants explained that they had found the property listed online, contacted the alleged landlord, and sent a deposit and the first month's rent via cash app. Surprisingly, they remained polite throughout the conversation.

At this property, we already had a procedure for dealing with squatters. After listening to their side of the story, I presented their options. First, they could choose to stay in the property, but this would involve reapplying and repaying all the necessary fees. This process included credit checks for all adults over 18, application fees, and background checks. They also needed to provide proof of employment, with residency not guaranteed until after a successful application.

The second option was to vacate the property, with a grace period of up to two weeks, provided they submitted their intent in writing. Lastly, I informed them about the eviction process in the state of Nevada if they chose not to legally rent the apartment. Fortunately, we were able to secure their residency, and they decided to remain in the home. Although we couldn't offer them any additional concessions or compensation, they did take advantage of an existing discount available for the property.

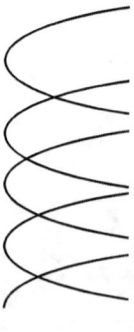

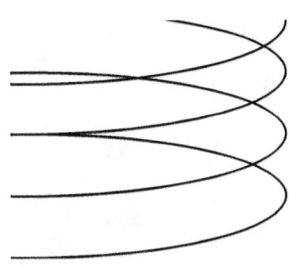

SCENARIO 1: A FRAUDULENT LEASE - CASESTUDY

One Monday, our customer service team alerted me to a resident's complaint regarding access to amenities in a property managed by a community association...
After the call, I initiated the following actions:

BEFORE MAKING THIS CALL, I HAD TAKEN THE FOLLOWING STEPS TO PREPARE:

1. Verified the rental amount.
2. Checked for any pending applications.
3. Created a move-in cost breakdown sheet detailing all associated fees.
4. Reviewed the timeline for our eviction process.
5. Prepared a comprehensive breakdown of the eviction process.

AFTER THE CALL, I INITIATED THE FOLLOWING ACTIONS:

1. Prepared a notice to be filed with the court (Note: If you are not a licensed property manager or comfortable with legal procedures, seeking an attorney's assistance is advisable).
2. Sent an email immediately after the conversation, summarizing what we had discussed and requesting a reply within 48 hours.
3. Set a calendar date for a follow-up with the resident.

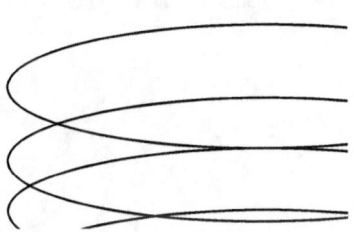

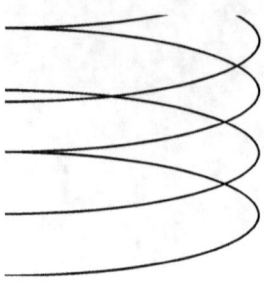

SCENARIO 1: A FRAUDULENT LEASE - CASESTUDY

LESSONS LEARNED

Lessons Learned experiences shared in the previous sections, we've encountered the intricate challenges that come with managing unauthorized occupants in the realm of property management. These scenarios shed light on the complexities of balancing the interests of property owners, the public, and tenants. In this chapter, we'll delve into the invaluable lessons learned from these experiences:

1. Vigilance is Key:

One of the crucial lessons from the scenarios presented is the importance of vigilance. Unauthorized occupants can slip through the cracks, whether they are squatters or individuals who have fallen prey to fraudulent leases. Those responsible for managing properties must maintain constant vigilance in monitoring tenant rosters, applications, and occupancy to ensure the integrity of the property and protect the interests of the property owner.

2. Transparent Communication:

Transparency is essential when dealing with unauthorized occupants. Open and honest communication can help occupants understand their options, responsibilities, and the potential consequences of their actions. By being clear about the eviction process, the legal framework, and the timeline involved, those responsible for managing properties can foster a sense of fairness for all parties involved.

3. Equitable Solutions:

In each scenario, we strived to find equitable solutions. The goal was not only to protect the interests of the property owner but also to offer options to unauthorized occupants. Whether they chose to remain and go through the proper application process or vacate the property, the focus was on providing choices that respected both the rights of tenants and the property owner.

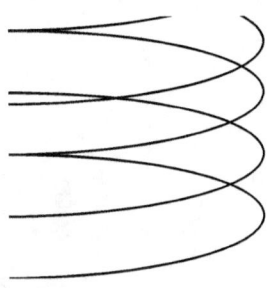

SCENARIO 1: A FRAUDULENT LEASE - CASESTUDY

LESSONS LEARNED

14. Preparedness and Due Diligence:

Preparation is paramount when dealing with unauthorized occupants. The steps taken before, during, and after the initial contact with the occupants were meticulously planned. Those responsible for managing properties should be well-prepared, from verifying property records to outlining eviction processes, setting clear deadlines, and maintaining transparent communication.

5. Balancing Fiduciary Duties:

Those responsible for managing properties have a fiduciary duty to property owners, but they also bear responsibilities to the public, including potential tenants. Balancing these dual duties is a crucial aspect of property management. Finding a harmonious equilibrium that respects both parties' interests can be challenging but is essential for maintaining trust and integrity in the industry.

6. Legal Expertise:

In some cases, it may be necessary to seek legal expertise, especially when navigating complex eviction procedures. Those responsible for managing properties who are not licensed property managers or who are not comfortable handling legal aspects should consider consulting an attorney to ensure that all actions taken are within the bounds of the law.

The experiences recounted in this chapter illustrate the multifaceted nature of property management and the various considerations that must be addressed when managing unauthorized occupants. By heeding the lessons learned from these experiences, those responsible for managing properties can better navigate this sensitive and challenging aspect of the industry, ultimately working toward a harmonious and equitable resolution for all parties involved.

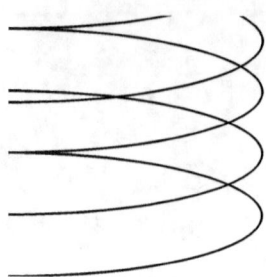

SCENARIO 1: A FRAUDULENT LEASE - CASESTUDY

EXTRA SECTION: ENSURING TRANSPARENCY IN THE EVICTION PROCESS

Following the email reply from the unauthorized occupants, stating their intent to remain in the property, I promptly responded with comprehensive information about the property and provided them with a link to our application site. I wanted to make sure they understood the complete leasing process as if they were entirely new residents.

Transparency is a core principle in property management, especially when dealing with eviction processes, as I outline in my book titled "Collections." This transparency not only benefits the property owner but also ensures that tenants are well-informed about their responsibilities and options.

In my communication with the unauthorized occupants, I provided the following details:

1. **Filing Date:** I specified the date when we would file with the court, making them aware of the legal steps involved.

2. **Additional Fees:** I outlined the day when additional fees would be added to their account and the duration during which they had to pay these fees.

3. **Court Dates:** I informed them about the court dates and any necessary appearances, ensuring they were fully aware of the legal proceedings.

4. **Reminders:** I mentioned that we would send out reminders to help them stay on top of important dates and deadlines.

In the property management industry, it is crucial to maintain a balance that benefits both property owners and tenants. Owners seek to receive their rightful payments, while tenants are looking for a stable place to call home. By providing tenants with options and clear communication, we strive to achieve this balance. All funds contributed to resolving any negative balance ultimately benefit the property owner, helping maintain the property and ensuring a quality living environment for tenants.

By maintaining open and honest communication throughout the eviction process, we aim to find a fair and mutually beneficial resolution for all parties involved in this sensitive industry. Transparency and diligence in our operations are key to ensuring that property management remains a trusted and reliable service for both property owners and residents.

CHAPTER N.3

Chapter : 4
Step-by-step guide
for identifying
unauthorized
occupants.

- Identifying unauthorized occupants
- Communication and notification procedures
- Conflict resolution strategies

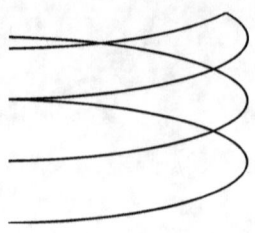

CHAPTER 4: STEP-BY-STEP GUIDE FOR IDENTIFYING UNAUTHORIZED OCCUPANTS.

Step 1: Regular Lease Review
- Periodic Lease Audits: Conduct regular audits of lease agreements to ensure they accurately reflect the authorized occupants. These audits can be done annually or at the time of lease renewal.
- Notification: Inform tenants about the upcoming lease review well in advance. Frame it as a standard procedure to update lease records and confirm everyone's safety and well-being.

Step 2: Monitor Lease Expirations
- Lease Expiry Reminders: Provide tenants with lease expiration reminders well before their lease is due for renewal. This serves as a gentle nudge for tenants to notify you of any changes in occupancy.
- Ease of Renewal: Make lease renewal processes as convenient as possible, encouraging tenants to inform you about any changes in occupancy at that time.

Step 3: Utility Usage Analysis
- Utility Bill Review: Periodically review utility bills for significant fluctuations. Unexplained increases in utility consumption may indicate additional, unauthorized occupants.
- Friendly Inquiry: Reach out to the tenant in question with a friendly inquiry. Frame it as a way to help them with potential utility savings by ensuring the right number of occupants is on the lease.

Step 4: Routine Property Inspections
- Scheduled Inspections: Implement scheduled property inspections that focus on safety and fire hazards, as well as general property maintenance.
- Observation: During these inspections, pay attention to any signs of increased occupancy, such as additional belongings, changes in living conditions, or unfamiliar individuals on the premises.

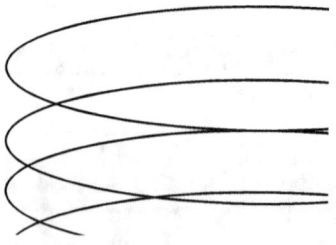

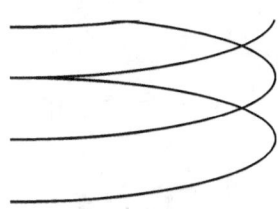

CHAPTER 4: STEP-BY-STEP GUIDE FOR IDENTIFYING UNAUTHORIZED OCCUPANTS.

Step 5: Respectful Communication
- Friendly Conversation: If you suspect unauthorized occupancy, initiate a non-confrontational conversation with the tenant. Approach it as a friendly discussion about maintaining a safe and pleasant living environment.
- Inform and Offer Solutions: Begin with a considerate introduction, such as, "Hello, I've been informed that there might be someone in your unit who is not on the lease." Offer a solution by saying, "If you'd like, we can help you add them to the lease. They just need to fill out an application and pay the application fee."
- Lease Violation Clarity: Clearly explain which part of their lease they are potentially violating and how adding the person to the lease can remedy the issue. Provide a timeline and guide them through the process.

By following these non-controversial steps, property managers can identify unauthorized occupants while maintaining a respectful and helpful approach, often resolving issues without the need for more confrontational measures. This not only saves property owners potential expenses but also fosters positive tenant relationships.

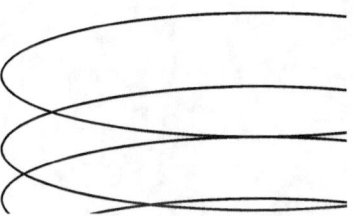

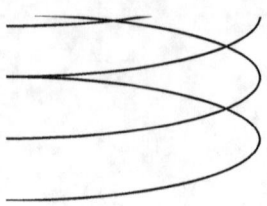

CHAPTER 4A: COMMUNICATION AND NOTIFICATION PROCEDURES FOR UNAUTHORIZED OCCUPANTS

In the challenge of managing unauthorized occupants, effective communication and notification procedures are essential for a harmonious resolution. This chapter outlines five detailed techniques for non-confrontational and respectful communication in handling unauthorized occupants.

Technique 1: Friendly and Informative Initial Contact
Example: Start with a polite and informative approach, "Hello, we've received some information about potential unauthorized occupants in your unit. We'd like to discuss this with you to ensure the safety and well-being of all residents."

Technique 2: Offer Clear Solutions
Example: Provide practical options, "If it turns out there are unauthorized occupants, we can help you add them to the lease. They just need to fill out an application and pay the application fee."

Technique 3: Notify in Writing After Discussion
Example: Summarize the conversation in a written notice, "Following our discussion, we wanted to confirm the potential lease violation and the steps to rectify the situation. Please find this information in written form for your reference."

Technique 4: Set Up a Clear Timeline
Example: "We understand that it may take some time to address this situation. We're here to guide you through the process. Let's establish a clear timeline for adding any unauthorized occupants to the lease or addressing the issue."

Technique 5: Reminder and Follow-Up
Example: Send a friendly reminder, if necessary, "As we approach the agreed-upon timeline for addressing the unauthorized occupants, we wanted to check in and ensure that everything is progressing smoothly. If you have any questions or need assistance, feel free to reach out."

By implementing these techniques, property managers can maintain a considerate and effective communication approach, fostering a positive atmosphere for addressing unauthorized occupants while minimizing potential disputes and complications.

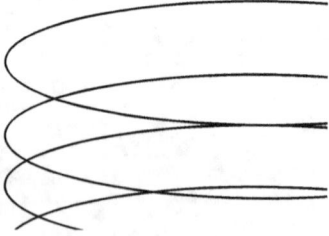

Chapter: 4bConflict resolution strategies

- Chapter: 4b Conflict Resolution Techniques for Unauthorized Occupants

Dealing with unauthorized occupants in property management can be a complex and sensitive issue. This chapter presents tangible and industry-standard conflict resolution techniques, specifically tailored to various scenarios involving unauthorized occupants. These techniques aim to resolve conflicts while maintaining a positive and professional relationship with tenants.

Scenario 1: Squatters - Legal Notice and Police Involvement
- Technique 1: When dealing with squatters, it's crucial to serve them with a legal notice that clearly establishes the property's ownership and your intent to involve law enforcement. Contact the local police to handle the eviction, ensuring you adhere to all legal procedures.

Scenario 2: Rental Scam Victims - Verification of Tenant Status
- Technique 2: For individuals who have been scammed and may not be aware of their tenant status, conduct a thorough verification to confirm their status through official documentation or tenant databases. Provide them with guidance on the legal process for leasing the property while protecting them from further scams.

Scenario 3: Roommate Left Behind - Lease Amendment
- Technique 3: In cases where a roommate is left behind without being on the lease, consider offering a lease amendment. Suggest, "We can amend the lease to include the remaining roommate. They just need to complete an application and pay the application fee."

Scenario 4: Tenant's Desire to Stay - Application and Lease Update
- Technique 4: If the unauthorized occupant wishes to stay, guide them through the formal application process and the lease update. Encourage them to complete the application and ensure that the lease is updated to meet all terms and conditions.

Scenario 5: Tenant's Desire to Leave - Friendly Lease Termination
- Technique 5: When the unauthorized occupant expresses a desire to leave, work collaboratively on a lease termination process. Offer a mutual agreement to end the lease, providing a clear timeline for their departure and ensuring a smooth transition for all parties involved.

These conflict resolution techniques are designed to address the specific challenges presented by unauthorized occupants in different scenarios, helping property managers navigate these situations professionally and effectively while preserving positive tenant relations.

CHAPTER N.3

Chapter 5: Legal Aspects

- Legal rights and responsibilities of property owners and managers
- Eviction and court procedures
- Working with law enforcement

Chapter 5: Legal Aspects

Legal aspects pertaining to unauthorized occupants in a property can be complex, and they vary depending on local, state, and national laws. Here are some key points to consider:

Legal Rights and Responsibilities of Property Owners and Managers:

1.a. Property owners have the right to control and manage their property. This includes the right to determine who can occupy the premises. b. Property owners have a responsibility to maintain safe and habitable living conditions for tenants, whether they are authorized or unauthorized occupants. c. Property owners should have a clear lease or rental agreement that outlines the terms and conditions of occupancy.

HOMELESSNESS AND PROPERTY OCCUPANCY:

2.a. The issue of homelessness is a societal challenge, and the homeless population sometimes resorts to occupying vacant properties as a means of survival. Property owners must confront the delicate balance between protecting their property rights and addressing the humanitarian concerns associated with homelessness. Local governments often establish procedures for handling homelessness and may require property owners to follow specific protocols before eviction.

Working with Law Enforcement:

3.a. Property owners and managers can involve law enforcement when dealing with unauthorized occupants, especially if the occupants are causing disturbances, engaging in illegal activities, or refusing to leave. b. Law enforcement may assist in removing unauthorized occupants through the legal eviction process. Property owners should follow proper channels and not resort to self-help methods. c. Law enforcement may also be involved in cases where unauthorized occupants are trespassing or committing other criminal activities on the property.

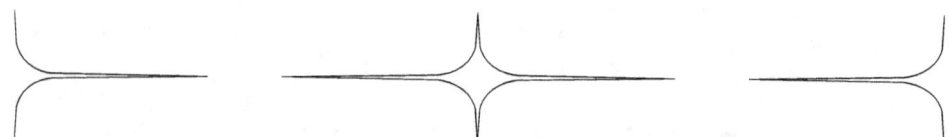

CONCLUSION:

It's essential for property owners and managers to be well-informed about the relevant laws and regulations in their area, as they can vary significantly. Consulting with legal counsel or local housing authorities is often advisable when dealing with unauthorized occupants to ensure that all actions taken are within the bounds of the law. Additionally, documentation of all interactions with unauthorized occupants, including notices and communications, can be crucial in legal proceedings.

CHAPTER N.6

Chapter 6. Resources for Escalation

- Legal resources
- Mediation and arbitration options
- Legal representation

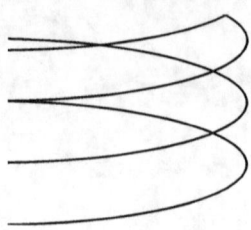

Chapter 6: Resources for Escalation

CHAPTER 6A: LEGAL RESOURCES:

LEGAL AID ORGANIZATIONS: ONLINE LEGAL DATABASES:

When dealing with escalation in legal matters, having access to the right resources is crucial. Here are some resources you can consider for each category:

1. - Many regions have legal aid organizations that provide free or low-cost legal assistance to individuals who cannot afford private representation. Examples include Legal Aid Society in the United States or Citizens Advice Bureau in the UK.

a. **Online Legal Databases: **
   - Platforms like LexisNexis or Westlaw provide comprehensive legal databases, statutes, and case law, offering valuable resources for legal research.

b. **Government Legal Services: **
   - Government legal services or ombudsman offices can provide information on legal rights and options. Check with your local or national government for available services.

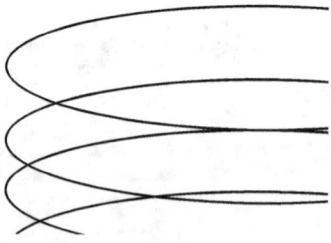

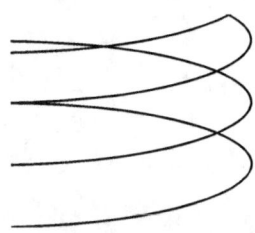

Chapter 6: Resources for Escalation

CHAPTER 6A: LEGAL RESOURCES:

LEGAL AID ORGANIZATIONS: 2. MEDIATION AND ARBITRATION OPTIONS:

When dealing with escalation in legal matters, having access to the right resources is crucial. Here are some resources you can consider for each category:

**2. Mediation and Arbitration Options: **
a. **Community Mediation Centers: **
- Many communities have mediation centers that offer services to help parties resolve disputes outside of court. These centers often have trained mediators who facilitate communication and negotiation.

b. **Arbitration Services: **
- Organizations like the American Arbitration Association (AAA) or the International Chamber of Commerce (ICC) provide arbitration services for resolving disputes without going to court.

c. **Online Dispute Resolution (ODR) Platforms: **
- Platforms such as Moria or Cybersettle offer online dispute resolution services, making it convenient for parties to resolve conflicts remotely.

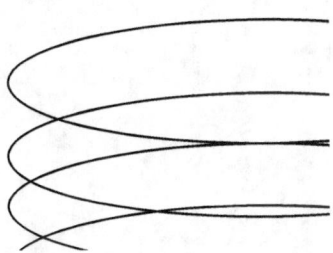

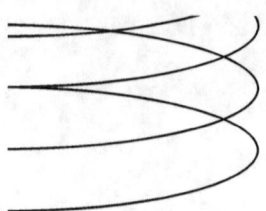

Chapter 6: Resources for Escalation

CHAPTER 6A: LEGAL RESOURCES: 3. LEGAL REPRESENTATION:

LEGAL AID ORGANIZATIONS:

When dealing with escalation in legal matters, having access to the right resources is crucial. Here are some resources you can consider for each category:

**3. Legal Representation: **
 a. **Local Bar Associations: **
 - Bar associations often provide directories of lawyers specializing in various areas of law. Contact your local bar association for recommendations.

 b. **Legal Clinics at Law Schools: **
 - Law school's often have legal clinics where law students, under the supervision of experienced attorneys, provide legal assistance to the community.

 c. **Private Attorneys: **
 - Seeking a private attorney who specializes in the relevant area of law is a common approach. Online platforms like Avvo or Martindale-Hubbell can help you find attorneys in your area.

Remember to research and choose resources based on your specific needs and the nature of the legal issue. Consulting with legal professionals and utilizing alternative dispute resolution methods can often lead to more efficient and cost-effective resolutions.

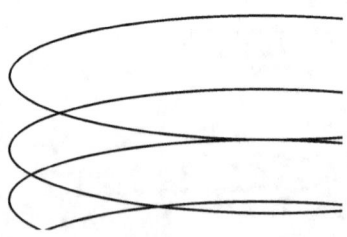

CHAPTER N.7

Chapter 7.
Effective
Communication

- Crafting effective emails and correspondence
- Communication templates

Chapter 7: Effective Communication:

CRAFTING EFFECTIVE EMAILS AND CORRESPONDENCE

7. Effective Communication

Crafting effective emails and correspondence
Effective email and correspondence crafting are a skill crucial for clear communication. It involves creating messages that are not only clear and concise but also tailored to the recipient's needs. This proficiency is cultivated through attention to detail, maintaining a professional tone, and considering the context of the communication. A well-structured email begins with a clear subject line, a polite salutation, and a brief introduction. The body of the email is characterized by its conciseness, clarity, and personalized touch. Correct grammar and spelling ensure the professionalism of the message. A call to action guides the recipient on the necessary steps, and a polite closing leaves a positive impression. With these elements in place, effective emails and correspondence contribute significantly to successful communication.

Chapter 7: Effective Communication:

SUPPORTING REASONS:

1. Clarity and Conciseness:
   - Clear and concise emails are more likely to be understood and acted upon promptly. A clutter-free message reduces the chances of misinterpretation and helps the recipient grasp the key information effortlessly.
2. Subject Line Significance:
   - A well-crafted subject line serves as a roadmap for the recipient, providing a quick overview of the email's content. This clarity aids in prioritizing and responding to messages efficiently.
3. Professional Tone:
   - Maintaining a professional tone establishes credibility and fosters a positive relationship with the recipient. Striking the right balance between formality and friendliness is key to effective communication.
4. Grammar and Spelling:
   - Correct grammar and spelling enhance the professionalism of the message. An error-free email reflects attention to detail and a commitment to delivering high-quality communication.
5. Personalization:
   - Personalizing emails demonstrates a genuine interest in the recipient and their needs. Addressing them by name and tailoring the content creates a connection, making the communication more engaging and relevant.
6. Call to Action Importance:
   - Clearly stating the desired action in an email guide, the recipient on what steps to take next. This clarity eliminates confusion and increases the likelihood of a prompt and accurate response.
7. Polite Closing Impact:
   - Ending an email with a polite closing adds a courteous touch to the communication. It leaves a positive impression and contributes to building a professional relationship with the recipient.
8. Responsive to Previous Correspondence:
   - Referencing previous correspondence demonstrates continuity and ensures that the email aligns with the ongoing conversation. This consideration for context enhances the effectiveness of the message.
9. Consideration of the Audience:
   - Tailoring the communication style to the audience is crucial. Understanding the recipient's preferences and expectations allows for a more targeted and impactful message.
10. Review Before Sending:
   - Taking a moment to review an email before sending is a crucial step. It allows for the correction of errors, ensures that the message aligns with its intended purpose, and contributes to the overall professionalism of the communication.

In conclusion, effective email and correspondence crafting involve a thoughtful integration of these elements, fostering clear, professional, and impactful communication.

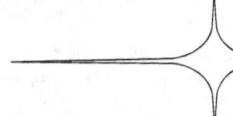

Chapter 7: Effective Communication: Communication templates

Effective communication lies at the heart of successful property management. In this chapter, we delve into the art of clear and impactful communication through the lens of email templates. These templates are provided as examples for your reference and are intended to be used with discretion in your specific property management context.

While these templates offer a foundation for crafting your messages, it's crucial to tailor them to the unique circumstances of each situation. Consider them as starting points that can be adapted to align with your communication style and the specifics of your property management agreements.

Additionally, it's important to note that if you have received legal notices or are dealing with legal matters, I strongly recommend seeking advice from a qualified attorney before initiating any further correspondence. Legal nuances may vary, and professional legal guidance ensures that your actions align with the specific legal requirements of your jurisdiction.

Now, let's explore some Email Templates that can help contribute to a seamless property management experience.

Chapter 7: Effective Communication: Communication templates

Issue 1: Occupied Abandoned Properties

Email 1: Initial Notice
Subject: Urgent: Occupancy Concern at [Property Address]

Dear [Property Owner/Responsible Party],

I hope this email finds you well. We have observed signs of occupancy at the property located at [Property Address], which is currently listed as abandoned. It's crucial that we address this issue promptly to ensure the safety and integrity of the property. Please let us know if you are aware of any authorized occupants or if you have any information regarding the current situation.

Thank you for your immediate attention to this matter.

Best regards,
[Your Name]
[Your Title]
[Contact Information]

Email 2: Conversation Overview with Options
Subject: Follow-up: Occupancy Concerns at [Property Address]

Dear [Property Owner/Responsible Party],

Following our previous communication, we would like to discuss the options available to address the occupancy concerns at [Property Address]. We understand the sensitive nature of this issue and want to work collaboratively to find a resolution.

Option 1: If you are aware of authorized occupants, please provide their contact information and any relevant documentation.

Option 2: If you are not aware of any authorized occupants, we recommend initiating an inspection to assess the situation and take necessary actions.

Please respond at your earliest convenience to indicate your preferred option or suggest an alternative course of action.

Thank you for your cooperation.

Best regards,
[Your Name]
[Your Title]
[Contact Information]

Chapter 7: Effective Communication: Communication templates

Email 3: Follow-up
Subject: Follow-up: Occupancy Concerns at [Property Address]

Dear [Property Owner/Responsible Party],

I hope this email finds you well. We wanted to follow up regarding the occupancy concerns at [Property Address]. Your prompt response is crucial in addressing this matter effectively.

If you have already provided information or taken action, we appreciate your cooperation. If not, please let us know the status or any additional details you can provide.

Thank you for your attention to this important issue.

Best regards,
[Your Name]
[Your Title]
[Contact Information]

Email 4: Advisement of Intent to Move Forward with Legal Proceedings
Subject: Final Notice: Legal Action Regarding Occupancy at [Property Address]

Dear [Property Owner/Responsible Party],

Despite our previous attempts to address the occupancy concerns at [Property Address], we have not received sufficient information or cooperation. Regrettably, we must advise you that if the matter remains unresolved within [specified timeframe], we will proceed with legal action to reclaim and secure the property.

We understand the gravity of this situation and sincerely hope to avoid legal proceedings. Please respond urgently with the necessary information or actions to prevent further escalation.

Thank you for your immediate attention.

Best regards,
[Your Name]
[Your Title]
[Contact Information]

Feel free to customize these templates based on the specific details of each situation.

CHAPTER N.8

Chapter 8. Preventing Unauthorized Occupancy

- Screening and background checks □
- Lease agreements and policies
- Security measures

Chapter 8. Preventing Unauthorized Occupancy

. Preventing Unauthorized Occupancy

In a landscape where property management demands vigilance and foresight, preventing unauthorized occupancy emerges as a paramount priority. This imperative is underscored by a myriad of reasons, including the safeguarding of property integrity, maintaining a secure living environment, and upholding legal compliance. Employing stringent screening and background checks during tenant selection forms the initial bulwark against unauthorized occupants. Clear and comprehensive lease agreements, coupled with effective policies, serve as a contractual framework that explicitly defines and enforces occupancy parameters. Concurrently, implementing robust security measures, from access control systems to community awareness initiatives, fortifies the defenses against unauthorized entry. By proactively addressing this challenge, property managers not only protect property assets but also nurture a harmonious and secure residential community.

LET'S DELVE INTO THE STRATEGIES FOR PREVENTING UNAUTHORIZED OCCUPANCY:

1. SCREENING AND BACKGROUND CHECKS

1. Screening and Background Checks:
Implementing thorough screening and background checks is a critical step in preventing unauthorized occupancy. This process involves:

- Rigorous Application Process: Design a comprehensive rental application that requires detailed information about prospective tenants, including rental history, employment, and references.
- Credit Checks: Conducting credit checks helps assess the financial responsibility of potential tenants, providing insights into their ability to meet financial obligations.
- Criminal Background Checks: Screen for criminal history to ensure the safety and well-being of the community and property.
- Rental History Verification: Contacting previous landlords helps verify the applicant's rental history and ensures they have a positive track record.
- Employment Verification: Confirming employment details helps assess the stability of the tenant's income.

Chapter 8. Preventing Unauthorized Occupancy

2. Lease Agreements and Policies:

Crafting clear and comprehensive lease agreements, along with effective policies, is instrumental in preventing unauthorized occupancy. This involves:

- Detailed Lease Agreements: Ensure that lease agreements explicitly outline who is permitted to reside on the property. Clearly state the names of authorized occupants and restrict any subletting without prior written consent.
- Occupancy Limits: Define and enforce occupancy limits based on local regulations and property size. Clearly communicate these limits in the lease agreement.
- Regular Lease Reviews: Periodically review lease agreements to ensure they align with current occupants. Promptly update agreements to reflect any changes in occupancy.
- Notification Policies: Establish policies requiring tenants to notify the property management of any changes in occupancy. This ensures timely updates and prevents unauthorized residents.
- Strict Enforcement: Clearly communicate consequences for unauthorized occupancy in lease agreements. Enforce these policies consistently to maintain a secure and compliant community.

3. SECURITY MEASURES:

Implementing robust security measures is essential to deter unauthorized occupants and maintain a safe living environment. This includes:

- Access Control Systems: Install secure access control systems for entry points, limiting access to authorized individuals. This may include key cards, electronic fobs, or secure keypads.
- Surveillance Cameras: Strategically place surveillance cameras in common areas and entrances to monitor and record activities, acting as a deterrent against unauthorized entry.
- Regular Inspections: Conduct regular property inspections to ensure compliance with occupancy policies. This proactive approach helps identify and address potential issues before they escalate.
- Community Awareness: Foster a sense of community awareness among residents, encouraging them to report any suspicious activity or unauthorized individuals to the property management.
- Collaboration with Law Enforcement: Establish communication channels with local law enforcement to report and address unauthorized occupancy promptly.

By combining these preventative measures, property managers can create a secure and well-regulated living environment, minimizing the risk of unauthorized occupancy and maintaining the integrity of the community.

CHAPTER N.9

Chapter 9. Case Studies

- Additional real-life examples and their resolutions

Chapter 9. Case Studies

Additional real-life examples and their resolutions

Welcome to Chapter 9, a rich compilation of real-life case studies that delve into the intricate challenges posed by unauthorized occupants in the realm of property management. This section goes beyond theory, offering you tangible narratives of property managers navigating through complex scenarios. Each case study is accompanied by a step-by-step guide, providing you with practical insights and actionable steps to tackle similar challenges.

These case studies encapsulate the dynamic nature of unauthorized occupancy issues, illustrating the multifaceted aspects of identification, communication, and resolution. From fraudulent leases to unexpected squatters, each scenario unfolds a unique set of challenges that property managers must navigate with finesse.

As we immerse ourselves in these case studies, consider them as real-world classrooms, where you not only witness the challenges but also discover effective strategies for resolution. The accompanying step-by-step guides are designed to be your navigational tool, offering a clear path to addressing unauthorized occupants in your own property management endeavors.

Let's embark on this journey, where theory meets practice, and learn from the experiences of seasoned property managers who have successfully navigated the complexities of unauthorized occupancy.

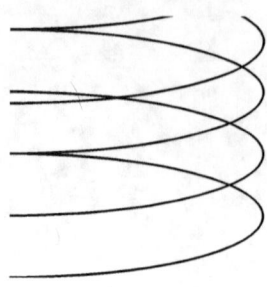

SCENARIO 1: DEALING WITH A PERSISTENT SQUATTER

Scenario 1: Dealing with a Persistent Squatter
Background
As a property manager, I faced a persistent squatter in one of our vacant properties. Despite numerous eviction attempts, the squatter repeatedly returned, making the eviction process a protracted ordeal.

Challenges
- The squatter had deep knowledge of the legal system, exploiting every possible delay tactic.
- Each eviction process involved an extensive legal battle, consuming time and resources.

Outcome
- After multiple eviction attempts and countless court appearances, the squatter was finally removed.
- The property management team implemented enhanced security measures to deter future unauthorized occupants.

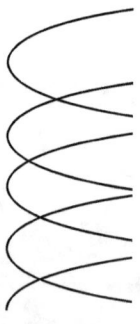

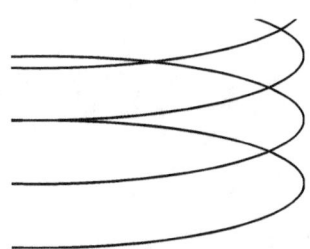

SCENARIO 1: DEALING WITH A PERSISTENT SQUATTER - CASESTUDY

Case Study 1: Persistent Squatter Eviction
Introduction

This case study highlights a property manager's struggle to evict a persistent squatter. The process involved multiple eviction attempts, legal battles, and lessons learned in dealing with determined unauthorized occupants.

Step-by-Step Guide: Dealing with Persistent Squatters

1. Initial Discovery and Assessment: Investigate the situation when unauthorized occupation is discovered. Document the property's condition, take photographs, and assess safety concerns.
2. Secure the Property: Secure the property immediately to prevent re-entry by the squatter. Change locks and secure entry points.
3. Consult Legal Counsel: Seek legal counsel with experience in landlord-tenant law, especially when dealing with persistent squatters. Understand your legal rights and responsibilities.
4. Notices and Documentation: Send eviction notices to the squatter, maintaining copies of all notices and communication.
5. Court Proceedings: If necessary, initiate legal proceedings by filing an unlawful detainer lawsuit. Present evidence, including photos and notices, in court.
6. Obtaining an Eviction Order: Once you have an eviction order from the court, obtain a writ of possession.
7. Enforce the Eviction: Work with local law enforcement to enforce the eviction and remove the squatter from the property.

Conclusion
Dealing with a persistent squatter requires determination, knowledge of legal procedures, and persistence in upholding property rights.

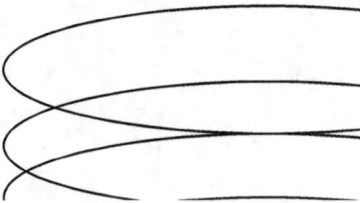

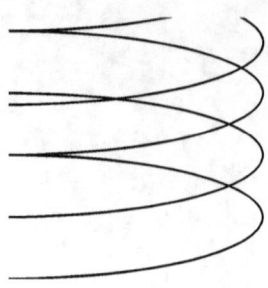

SCENARIO 2: RESOLVING AN UNAUTHORIZED OCCUPANT SITUATION

Scenario 2: Resolving an Unauthorized Occupant Situation
Background

As a landlord, I discovered an unauthorized occupant in my rental property. The occupant had moved in without my consent, creating a complex situation.

Challenges
- I had to navigate tenant rights while ensuring the unauthorized occupant was removed.
- Communication with the unauthorized occupant was strained, making resolution difficult.

Outcome
- Through legal action, I successfully had the unauthorized occupant evicted.
- The property was returned to me, and I implemented better lease agreements to prevent future unauthorized occupants.

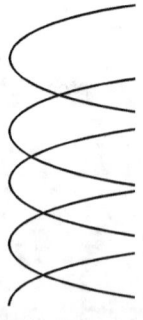

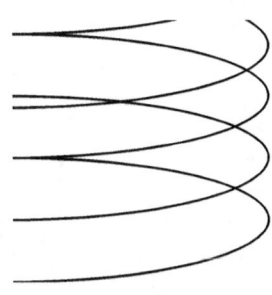

CASE STUDY SCENARIO 2: RESOLVING AN UNAUTHORIZED OCCUPANT SITUATION

This case study details a landlord's experience with an unauthorized occupant in their rental property, outlining the challenges and solutions to resolve the situation.

Step-by-Step Guide: Dealing with Unauthorized Occupants

1. Initial Discovery and Assessment: Investigate and assess the situation. Ensure the unauthorized occupant is not a legitimate tenant.
2. Review Lease Agreements: Check the lease agreements and tenant's rights. Unauthorized occupants often violate the lease agreement.
3. Communicate with Tenant: If there's a legitimate tenant involved, communicate with them to understand the situation. They may be unaware of the unauthorized occupant.
4. Send a Cure or Quit Notice: Issue a "cure or quit" notice to the tenant if they are aware of the unauthorized occupant but haven't taken action to remove them.
5. Consult Legal Counsel: Seek legal advice to ensure you're following local laws and regulations. Legal counsel can guide you through the eviction process.
6. Eviction Process: Follow the eviction process as guided by legal counsel. This typically involves court proceedings and obtaining an eviction order.
7. Enforce the Eviction: Work with law enforcement to enforce the eviction and remove the unauthorized occupant.

Conclusion
Resolving unauthorized occupant situations requires adherence to legal procedures, communication with tenants, and diligent action to protect your property rights.

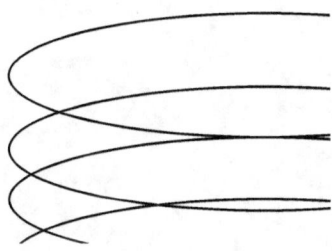

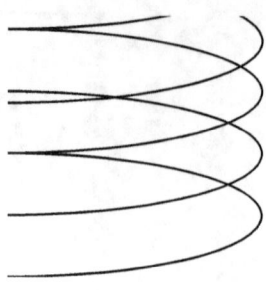

SCENARIO 3: DEALING WITH A SQUATTER IN A FORECLOSED PROPERTY

S
Background
As a real estate investor, I encountered an unexpected challenge when I purchased a foreclosed property. Upon arrival for an inspection, I discovered a squatter who had been living in the property for an extended period, a situation commonly faced by property buyers.

Challenges
- The squatter was not the former owner and had no legal claim to the property.
- Despite my legal ownership, removing the squatter required navigating complex laws and eviction procedures.

Outcome
- After successfully evicting the squatter through legal processes, the property was cleared for renovation and resale.
- I now conduct thorough property inspections before finalizing purchases to prevent such occurrences in the future.

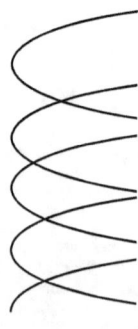

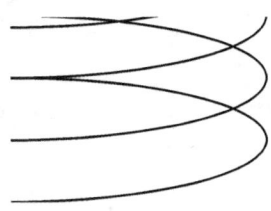

CASE STUDY 3: SQUATTER IN A FORECLOSED PROPERTY

This case study delves into the common scenario of encountering a squatter in a foreclosed property after its purchase. We will explore the challenges faced and the step-by-step process for removing the unauthorized occupant.

Step-by-Step Guide: Dealing with Squatters in Foreclosed Properties

- Initial Discovery and Assessment
    - When inspecting the foreclosed property, I discovered signs of occupation, such as personal belongings and makeshift living areas.
    - I documented the property's condition and took photographs as evidence of the squatter's presence.
- Review Ownership Documentation
    - I reviewed all ownership documents, ensuring that the property was legally mine and the former owner had no right to occupy it.
- Communication with Squatter
    - I initially attempted to communicate with the squatter to understand their situation. They claimed to have nowhere else to go.
- Send a Notice to Quit
    - As the squatter had no legal claim to the property, I sent a "notice to quit," giving them a specific period to vacate the premises.
- Consult Legal Counsel
    - I sought legal advice to confirm I was following the appropriate legal procedures. Legal counsel confirmed that I had the right to proceed with eviction.
- Eviction Process
    - I initiated the eviction process, which involved filing a formal eviction lawsuit and attending a court hearing.
    - I presented my case in court, providing evidence of ownership and the notice to quit served to the squatter.
- Enforce the Eviction
    - Following the court's decision, I obtained an eviction order. Law enforcement was involved to enforce the eviction, ensuring the squatter left the property.

Conclusion

This case study and guide highlight the challenges of encountering squatters in foreclosed properties and provide a comprehensive approach to removing them. By following the legal procedures, property buyers can protect their ownership rights and avoid costly delays in property renovation or resale.

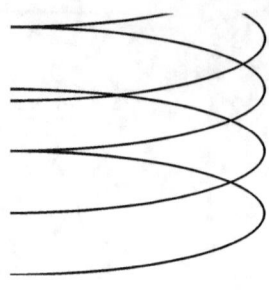

SCENARIO 4: UNAUTHORIZED OCCUPANTS IN A MULTIFAMILY RENTAL

Background

As a property manager for a multifamily rental complex, I faced an issue involving unauthorized occupants. A tenant had allowed family members to move in without notifying the management or updating the lease agreement, a common problem in multifamily housing.

Challenges

- The unauthorized occupants had been living in the unit for an extended period.
- Communicating with the original tenant was difficult, as they had initially denied the presence of the unauthorized occupants.

Outcome

- Through strict enforcement of lease agreements and legal procedures, the unauthorized occupants were removed, and the lease was updated.
- Regular property inspections and clear communication with tenants were implemented to prevent future unauthorized occupants.

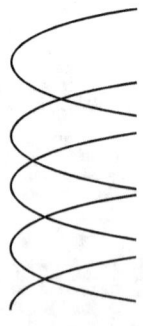

CASE STUDY 4: UNAUTHORIZED OCCUPANTS IN A MULTIFAMILY RENTAL

INTRODUCTION

This case study examines the issue of unauthorized occupants in a multifamily rental, focusing on the challenges faced and the step-by-step process for resolution.
Step-by-Step Guide: Dealing with Unauthorized Occupants in Multifamily Rentals

- Initial Discovery and Assessment
  - After receiving complaints from neighbors about overcrowding and noise, I investigated the unit and documented the presence of unauthorized occupants.
- Review Lease Agreements
  - Carefully reviewed the lease agreement to identify the legitimate tenant(s) and any restrictions on occupants.
- Communication with Tenant
  - Initiated a conversation with the original tenant, who initially denied the presence of unauthorized occupants.
  - After persistent communication, the tenant admitted that family members had moved in without notice.
- Send a Cure or Quit Notice
  - Issued a "cure or quit" notice, which demanded that the tenant either remove the unauthorized occupants or vacate the property.
- Consult Legal Counsel
  - Sought legal advice to ensure compliance with legal procedures and local laws, especially in multifamily housing scenarios.
- Eviction Process
  - Initiated the eviction process by filing necessary documents, which included a court hearing and the presentation of evidence.
- Enforce the Eviction
  - After obtaining an eviction order from the court, law enforcement was involved to enforce the eviction and remove the unauthorized occupants.

Conclusion

Addressing unauthorized occupants in multifamily rentals involves adherence to legal procedures, clear communication with tenants, and regular property inspections to maintain a peaceful living environment and protect property rights.

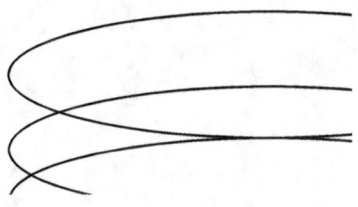

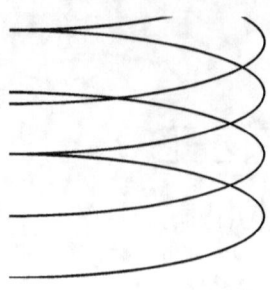

SCENARIO 5: UNAUTHORIZED OCCUPANT IN A DOMESTIC RELATIONSHIP

BACKGROUND

In my role as a property manager, I encountered a challenging situation involving an unauthorized occupant in a domestic relationship living in one of our rental units. The leaseholder had requested the unauthorized occupant to leave due to a deteriorating relationship. However, the unauthorized occupant refused, leading to a complex legal situation. The only legal recourse was to initiate eviction proceedings against both the leaseholder and the unauthorized occupant. This approach is grounded in the legal principle of established residency, which ensures that all occupants' rights are protected, even when they are not on the lease.

Challenges
- The leaseholder was paying rent and complying with the lease, making their eviction seem unjust.
- However, the unauthorized occupant had lived in the unit for an extended period and, according to legal standards, had established residency.

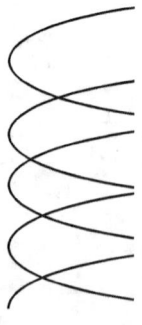

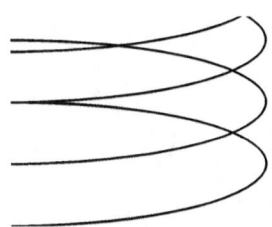

CASE STUDY 5: UNAUTHORIZED OCCUPANT IN A DOMESTIC RELATIONSHIP

Introduction
This case study illustrates the common yet legally complex scenario of dealing with an unauthorized occupant in a domestic relationship who refuses to leave a rental property. The case required both the leaseholder and the unauthorized occupant to be subject to eviction due to established residency rights.

Step-by-Step Guide: Dealing with Unauthorized Occupants in Domestic Relationships
Introduction
If you find yourself facing a situation similar to the case study involving an unauthorized occupant in a domestic relationship, follow this step-by-step guide to navigate the legal process effectively.

- Initial Discovery and Assessment
  - Begin by assessing the situation and documenting the circumstances surrounding the unauthorized occupant's presence.
  - Determine whether the unauthorized occupant has established residency in the property.
- Legal Consultation
  - Seek legal counsel with expertise in landlord-tenant law to understand the legal framework and options available.
- Communication with All Parties
  - Open lines of communication with both the leaseholder and the unauthorized occupant to discuss the situation and attempt to reach a voluntary resolution.
- Legal Evaluation
  - Have your legal counsel evaluate whether the unauthorized occupant has established residency based on local laws and regulations.
- Eviction Process
  - If it is legally determined that the unauthorized occupant has established residency, initiate the eviction process against both the leaseholder and the unauthorized occupant.
- Court Proceedings
  - File the necessary eviction paperwork, attend court hearings, and present your case with evidence supporting the need for eviction.
- Enforce the Eviction
  - After obtaining a court-issued eviction order, work with law enforcement to enforce the eviction, ensuring that both parties vacate the property.
  -

Conclusion
Dealing with unauthorized occupants in domestic relationships can be legally complex. This guide emphasizes the importance of legal counsel, understanding established residency rights, and the necessity of following proper eviction procedures to protect the rights of all parties involved.

CHAPTER N.10

Chapter 10.
Conclusion

- Recap of key takeaways
- Empowering homeowners and property managers
- Final words of advice

Chapter 10: Conclusion
Mastering the Art of Property Management

In the grand finale of our exploration into the labyrinth of property management, let's take a moment to savor the wisdom we've gathered and distill it into empowering insights for homeowners and property managers alike.

Recap of Key Takeaways:

Our journey commenced with the crucial foundation of legal understanding—a compass guiding us through the twists and turns of landlord-tenant laws. By establishing a solid grounding in legal principles, property managers are equipped to navigate the intricacies of property management with confidence and compliance.

We then refined the art of effective communication, transforming it into a powerful tool that not only conveys information but also builds bridges of clarity and connection. Recognizing the pivotal role communication plays in property management, we explored strategies for fostering positive relationships, addressing concerns, and navigating through complex scenarios with finesse.

Tackling the enigma of unauthorized occupancy, we uncovered a strategic roadmap for resolution. From preventive measures like thorough screening to effective communication strategies and conflict resolution techniques, our toolkit has expanded to ensure a methodical approach to overcoming the complexities associated with unauthorized occupants.

Real-life case studies painted vibrant illustrations, offering practical lessons in managing incidents with finesse. These narratives provided a firsthand glimpse into the challenges property managers face, illustrating the diverse scenarios and showcasing the application of our acquired knowledge in real-world contexts.

As we recap our journey, each milestone represents a building block in the construction of a comprehensive property management toolkit. The understanding of legal intricacies, the mastery of communication, the strategic approach to unauthorized occupancy, and the practical wisdom gleaned from case studies collectively form a robust foundation. Armed with these insights, property managers are better prepared to navigate the dynamic landscape of property management, fostering positive experiences for both landlords and tenants.

Empowering Homeowners and Property Managers:

Armed with this knowledge arsenal, you now wield a comprehensive set of tools to elevate your role as a homeowner or property manager. It goes beyond mere understanding; it's about putting this knowledge into strategic action.

Staying informed is not just a passive endeavor but an active commitment to ongoing education. The dynamic nature of the real estate landscape demands a continuous pursuit of knowledge. Regularly update yourself on legal changes, emerging trends, and industry best practices. This proactive approach ensures that you remain ahead of the curve and well-prepared for any shifts in the property management terrain.

Communication becomes a precision instrument in your hands. It's not just about conveying information but about doing so with purpose and clarity. Foster an environment of transparent and open communication with tenants, property owners, and other stakeholders. This not only builds trust but also contributes to a positive and cooperative atmosphere.

However, when the terrain gets tricky, remember that seeking legal counsel is a prudent and necessary step. The legal intricacies of property management can be intricate, and having a qualified attorney by your side ensures that you navigate these complexities with confidence and compliance. Whether it's drafting agreements, addressing disputes, or handling evictions, legal advice is a crucial ally.

Tackling challenges with a healthy dose of empathy is the cornerstone of effective property management. Understand the concerns and perspectives of both homeowners and tenants. By approaching situations with empathy, you create a space for constructive dialogue and collaborative problem-solving.

These strategies are not just principles; they form the bedrock of a robust and triumphant property management journey. The empowered homeowner or property manager is not just knowledgeable but proactive, communicative, legally savvy, and empathetic. By integrating these principles into your daily practices, you're not just managing properties; you're cultivating positive living experiences and contributing to the overall success of the communities you serve.

Final Words of Advice:
Words of Encouragement:

Final Words of Advice:

As you venture forth into the ongoing odyssey of property management, consider adaptability your staunchest ally. In the ever-shifting landscape of real estate, where challenges and opportunities seamlessly intertwine, the ability to adapt ensures not only your triumph but also a journey filled with fulfillment and enrichment.

Foster strong networks with fellow property managers, legal professionals, and industry experts. Collaborative partnerships often provide insights, support, and innovative solutions. Meticulously document each step of your property management processes. This not only serves as a comprehensive record but also acts as a valuable resource for future reference.

Strive for a delicate balance between unwavering firmness and compassionate understanding. Property management involves a nuanced interplay of rules and relationships. By maintaining a firm stance on legal and procedural matters while embracing empathy, you cultivate positive connections with tenants and property owners.

Continual improvement is the mantra that propels your success. Regularly reassess and refine your strategies, staying attuned to industry developments. This commitment to growth ensures that you not only navigate challenges effectively but also elevate the overall quality of your property management practices.

Words of Encouragement:

As you navigate the intricate dance of decisions in property management, remember that there's no one-size-fits-all formula. Each choice you make contributes to the unique canvas of your journey. Embrace the truth that, within the confines of the law, thoughtful decision-making is an art.

Trust yourself, adapt as needed within legal boundaries, and savor the satisfaction of mastering the art of property management. Your ability to shape your property management destiny rests in your capable hands. Approach your duties with diligence, following legal guidelines, and revel in the creative autonomy that thoughtful decision-making affords.

Here's to your continued success, always within the bounds of the law, and the exciting endeavors that await you! Cheers to your property management prowess!

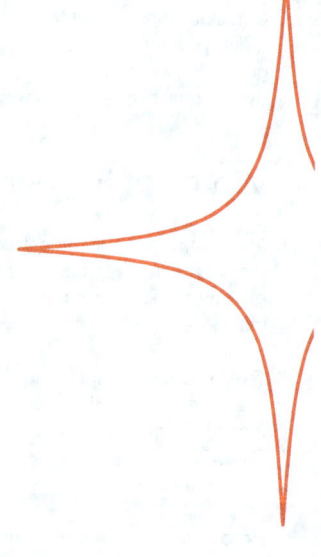

Appendices

- Sample documents (e.g., notices, lease clauses) □
- Glossary of legal terms
- Additional resources

Appendices: Sample documents (e.g., notices, lease clauses)

While I can provide some sample language for notices and lease clauses related to unauthorized occupants, it's important to note that these documents should be tailored to comply with local and state laws. Consulting with an attorney or a legal expert to ensure their legality and suitability for your specific situation is highly recommended. Here are some sample documents:

Appendices: Sample Unauthorized Occupant Notice:

[Your Company Letterhead] [Date]
[Name of Tenant] [Address of the Rental Property] [City, State, ZIP Code]
Re: Unauthorized Occupants at [Property Address]

Dear [Tenant's Name],

I hope this letter finds you well. We are writing to bring to your attention a matter of significant concern regarding your tenancy at the above-mentioned rental property.
It has come to our attention that there are individuals residing in the property who are not listed on the lease agreement and have not been approved as authorized occupants. This constitutes a breach of the lease agreement you signed, which clearly stipulates that only the individuals listed on the lease may reside in the property. Unauthorized occupants pose a risk to the property's safety, insurance coverage, and the overall well-being of the community.

We kindly request that you provide us with the necessary information regarding these unauthorized occupants, including their names, relationships, and the duration of their stay. It is imperative that we receive this information within [a reasonable period, e.g., 7 days] to ensure compliance with the lease terms.
If these unauthorized occupants are to be included in the lease, they must complete the application process, undergo the required background checks, and be approved by the property management.

Failure to comply with this request within the stipulated timeframe may result in further legal action, including eviction proceedings, to enforce the terms of the lease agreement. We understand that circumstances can change, and we are committed to working with you to ensure a lawful and harmonious tenancy. Please feel free to contact our office to discuss this matter further or to seek clarification on the required steps.
Sincerely,

[Your Name] [Your Title] [Your Contact Information]

Appendices: Sample Unauthorized Occupant Lease Clause:

:

This sample lease clause can be included in your lease agreement to address unauthorized occupants:

Unauthorized Occupants: The Tenant acknowledges that only the individuals listed in this lease agreement are authorized to reside in the leased property. Any other persons who wish to occupy the property must obtain prior written consent from the Landlord. Unauthorized occupants, not listed in this lease agreement and lacking Landlord's written consent, shall be considered in breach of this agreement. The Tenant is responsible for notifying the Landlord of any intended occupant changes and for ensuring that all occupants complete the necessary application process, including background checks, and are approved by the Landlord. Failure to adhere to this provision may result in eviction proceedings.

Please consult with a legal professional to ensure that this clause complies with your local and state laws and is suitable for your specific lease agreement.

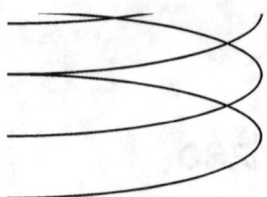

APPENDICES : GLOSSARY OF LEGAL TERMS

here's a glossary of some legal terms commonly used in property management:

1. Lease Agreement: A legally binding contract between a landlord (property owner) and a tenant that outlines the terms and conditions of renting a property.
2. Fair Housing Laws: Federal and state laws that prohibit discrimination based on factors such as race, color, religion, sex, national origin, disability, and familial status in housing and property management.
3. Eviction: The legal process of removing a tenant from a rental property due to lease violations, non-payment of rent, or other valid reasons.
4. Notice to Quit: A written notice served to a tenant to inform them of a lease violation or other grounds for eviction, typically specifying a deadline for compliance or vacating the property.
5. Landlord: The property owner who leases or rents out a property to tenants.
6. Tenant: An individual or entity who rents or leases a property from a landlord.
7. Lease Termination: The end of a lease or rental agreement, either upon its natural expiration or due to early termination.
8. Security Deposit: A sum of money paid by the tenant to the landlord at the beginning of the lease to cover potential damages, unpaid rent, or other financial obligations.
9. Lease Renewal: The process of extending a lease agreement for an additional period, typically with adjusted terms and conditions.
10. Tenant Screening: The process of evaluating prospective tenants through background checks, credit checks, and reference checks to assess their suitability for a rental property.
11. Rent Arrears: Unpaid rent that a tenant owes to the landlord.
12. Lease Violation: Breach of the terms and conditions outlined in the lease agreement, which can lead to eviction or other legal actions.
13. Property Management Agreement: A contract between a property owner and a property management company detailing the scope of property management services provided.
14. Rent Control: A set of regulations imposed by local or state governments to limit rent increases and protect tenants from excessive rent hikes.
15. Tenant Rights: Legal protections and entitlements that tenants have, including the right to a safe and habitable living environment and freedom from discrimination.
16. Mediation: A method of resolving disputes through a neutral third party who facilitates communication and negotiation between parties to reach an agreement.
17. Arbitration: A dispute resolution process in which an impartial third party makes a binding decision to resolve a conflict.
18. Sublease: A legal arrangement where a tenant rent all or part of their leased space to another party, with the original tenant retaining responsibility for the lease.
19. Property Inspection: A process in which the condition of a property is assessed, typically before a tenant moves in and after they move out, to document any damages or needed repairs.
20. Notice to Vacate: A written notice provided by the landlord or tenant, depending on the situation, to inform the other party of their intent to terminate the lease agreement and vacate the property.

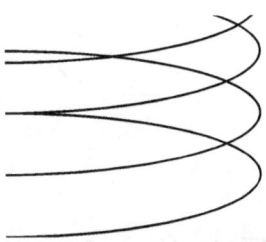

APPENDICES : ADDITIONAL RESOURCES - SAMPLE EMAILS

Sample Unauthorized Occupant Notice - Issue 1: Lessee Has Vacated the Property

[Your Company Letterhead] [Date]
[Name of Unauthorized Occupant] [Address of the Rental Property] [City, State, ZIP Code]

Re: Vacation of Rental Property - Unauthorized Occupant Notice

Dear [Name of Unauthorized Occupant],

I hope this letter finds you well. We are writing to inform you of a significant change in the tenancy at the above-mentioned rental property. As of [date], the lessee, [Name of Lessee], has vacated the property.

This notice serves to inform you that, in accordance with the lease agreement and the terms outlined therein, all unauthorized occupants are required to vacate the premises within [a reasonable notice period, e.g., 14 days] from the date of this notice. Your presence in the property is in violation of the lease agreement, which specifies that only the individuals listed on the lease are authorized to reside on the premises.

We kindly request your full cooperation in this matter. Failure to vacate the property within the stipulated timeframe may result in further legal action, including eviction proceedings, to enforce the terms of the lease agreement. We understand that circumstances may change, and should you wish to seek approval as a lawful occupant, please do not hesitate to contact our office to initiate the application process.
Sincerely,
[Your Name] [Your Title] [Your Contact Information]

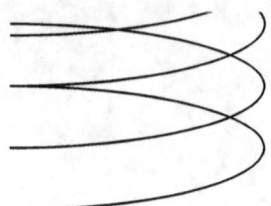

APPENDICES : ADDITIONAL RESOURCES - SAMPLE EMAILS

*Sample Unauthorized Occupant Notice - Issue 2: Unauthorized Occupant Requests Application Process

[Your Company Letterhead] [Date]
[Name of Unauthorized Occupant] [Address of the Rental Property] [City, State, ZIP Code]

Re: Application Process for Unauthorized Occupant - Notice to Complete or Vacate

Dear [Name of Unauthorized Occupant],

I hope this letter finds you well. We have received your request to complete the application process for your occupancy at the above-mentioned rental property. We appreciate your proactive approach in addressing this matter.

To ensure compliance with the terms of the lease agreement, we are pleased to inform you that we will gladly consider your application for authorized occupancy.

To initiate this process, please provide us with the following information and documents:
- Completed Rental Application for [Name of Unauthorized Occupant].
- A valid government-issued photo identification.
- Proof of income and employment.
- Consent for a background and credit check.
- Any other documentation required by the property management.

We kindly request that you submit these materials to our office within [a reasonable period, e.g., 7 days] from the date of this notice. Once we have received and reviewed your application, we will notify you of the approval status.

Failure to comply with this request and complete the application process within the stipulated timeframe may result in eviction proceedings, as your presence on the property is considered a violation of the lease agreement.

Should you have any questions or require further assistance, please do not hesitate to contact our office. We appreciate your cooperation in this matter and look forward to working with you to resolve this issue.

Sincerely,
[Your Name] [Your Title] [Your Contact Information]

APPENDICES : EXTRA SECTION: EXAMPLE OF CORRESPONDENCE INVOLVED

step-by-step list of all correspondence involved in the process of dealing with unauthorized occupants in a domestic relationship:

1. Initial Communication with Leaseholder
   - Initial communication begins with discussing the presence of the unauthorized occupant and the leaseholder's desire for them to leave.
2. Notice to Quit
   - Issue a "notice to quit" to both the leaseholder and the unauthorized occupant, specifying the required timeframe for them to vacate the property.
3. Legal Consultation
   - Consult with legal counsel to understand the legal framework in your jurisdiction and evaluate the legal status of the unauthorized occupant.
4. Follow-up Communication with Leaseholder and Unauthorized Occupant
   - Maintain ongoing communication with both parties to check for willingness to resolve the situation voluntarily.
5. Mediation Services Offer
   - If both parties are willing, offer mediation services to facilitate a peaceful resolution without legal action.
6. Eviction Notice
   - If mediation fails and the unauthorized occupant refuses to leave, issue an eviction notice, reiterating the necessity of their departure.
7. Filing Eviction Lawsuit
   - Begin the legal process by filing an eviction lawsuit in your local court against both the leaseholder and the unauthorized occupant.
8. Court Hearing Notices
   - Correspondence regarding court hearing dates and times will be sent to both parties.
9. Court Proceedings
   - Attend court hearings and provide evidence to support the eviction case. Legal correspondence and court documents will be shared during this phase.
10. Eviction Order
    - After winning the case, an eviction order will be issued by the court.
11. Enforcement of Eviction
    - Coordinate with law enforcement to enforce the eviction order, ensuring that both parties vacate the property.
12. Post-Eviction Correspondence
    - Notify both the leaseholder and the unauthorized occupant of the completion of the eviction process and discuss property restoration and return of any security deposits or belongings.
13. Property Restoration
    - Communicate any necessary details regarding property restoration, which may include inspections, cleaning, or repairs.

Throughout this process, it's crucial to maintain accurate records of all correspondence, including notices, emails, letters, and any legal documents. These records serve as crucial evidence of your compliance with legal procedures and your communication with all parties involved.

APPENDICES : EXTRA SECTION: EVICTION PROCESS

The duration of the eviction process for squatters varies from state to state in the United States, and it can depend on local laws, court procedures, and the specific circumstances of the case. I'll provide a general overview of the eviction process and some approximate time frames, but keep in mind that these are not definitive and can vary.

Standard Practices:

1. **Notice to Quit:** The process often begins with the property owner or landlord serving a notice to quit or vacate the premises. The length of this notice period can vary by state but typically ranges from 3 days to 30 days.
2. **Filing an Unlawful Detainer Lawsuit:** If the squatter does not leave after the notice period, the property owner can file an unlawful detainer lawsuit in court.
3. **Court Proceedings:** The court schedules a hearing, and both parties present their cases. The judge then issues an eviction order if warranted.
4. **Writ of Possession:** After obtaining an eviction order, the property owner can request a writ of possession, which allows law enforcement to remove the squatter from the property.

Standard Time Frames:

- **3 to 30 Days:** The initial notice to quit period.
- **2 to 6 Weeks:** Court proceedings, including the time it takes for a hearing and issuance of the eviction order.
- **Varies:** The time it takes to obtain a writ of possession and carry out the physical eviction.

Please note that these are rough estimates and can vary significantly. It's crucial to consult with a legal professional in your specific state for detailed information on eviction procedures and timelines, as laws and practices can differ. Additionally, each state has its own specific laws and procedures related to eviction, so it's important to research and understand your state's laws.

To find information on eviction laws and procedures in your individual state, you can typically start by contacting your state's housing or tenant-landlord authority or consult with a local attorney who specializes in landlord-tenant law. They can provide guidance specific to your state's regulations and practices.

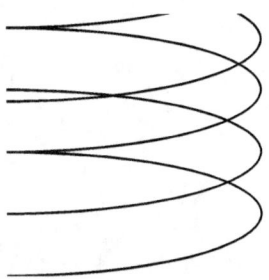

CHAPTER 9. CASE STUDIES

**EXTRA SECTION: STEP-BY-STEP GUIDE: RESOLVING UNAUTHORIZED OCCUPANTS IN A DOMESTIC RELATIONSHIP

- Court Proceedings
    - Attend court hearings as required. Present your case, backed by evidence, supporting the necessity of eviction. Your attorney will guide you through this process.
- Obtain an Eviction Order
    - After winning the case in court, obtain a court-issued eviction order. This document grants law enforcement the authority to remove both the leaseholder and the unauthorized occupant.
- Enforce the Eviction
    - Work with law enforcement to enforce the eviction order, ensuring that both parties vacate the property.
- Property Restoration
    - After the eviction, ensure that the property is returned to a habitable condition for future occupants.
- Legal Compliance
    - Continue to work closely with your attorney to ensure that all legal procedures and requirements are met throughout the process.

Conclusion
Dealing with unauthorized occupants in domestic relationships can be challenging, both emotionally and legally. Following this step-by-step guide, seeking legal counsel, and maintaining open communication are crucial to resolving the situation while upholding your rights as a property owner. Remember that laws and procedures may vary by location, so it's essential to consult with a local attorney for tailored guidance.
    -

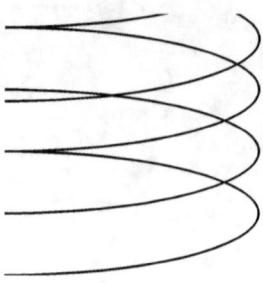

SCENARIO 1: A FRAUDULENT LEASE - CASESTUDY

LESSONS LEARNED

Lessons Learned experiences shared in the previous sections, we've encountered the intricate challenges that come with managing unauthorized occupants in the realm of property management. These scenarios shed light on the complexities of balancing the interests of property owners, the public, and tenants. In this chapter, we'll delve into the invaluable lessons learned from these experiences:

1. Vigilance is Key:

One of the crucial lessons from the scenarios presented is the importance of vigilance. Unauthorized occupants can slip through the cracks, whether they are squatters or individuals who have fallen prey to fraudulent leases. Those responsible for managing properties must maintain constant vigilance in monitoring tenant rosters, applications, and occupancy to ensure the integrity of the property and protect the interests of the property owner.

2. Transparent Communication:

Transparency is essential when dealing with unauthorized occupants. Open and honest communication can help occupants understand their options, responsibilities, and the potential consequences of their actions. By being clear about the eviction process, the legal framework, and the timeline involved, those responsible for managing properties can foster a sense of fairness for all parties involved.

3. Equitable Solutions:

In each scenario, we strived to find equitable solutions. The goal was not only to protect the interests of the property owner but also to offer options to unauthorized occupants. Whether they chose to remain and go through the proper application process or vacate the property, the focus was on providing choices that respected both the rights of tenants and the property owner.

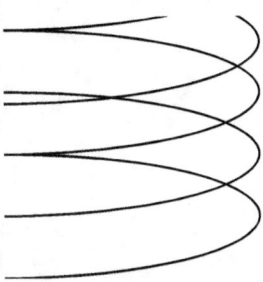

SCENARIO 1: A FRAUDULENT LEASE - CASESTUDY

LESSONS LEARNED

14. Preparedness and Due Diligence:

Preparation is paramount when dealing with unauthorized occupants. The steps taken before, during, and after the initial contact with the occupants were meticulously planned. Those responsible for managing properties should be well-prepared, from verifying property records to outlining eviction processes, setting clear deadlines, and maintaining transparent communication.

5. Balancing Fiduciary Duties:

Those responsible for managing properties have a fiduciary duty to property owners, but they also bear responsibilities to the public, including potential tenants. Balancing these dual duties is a crucial aspect of property management. Finding a harmonious equilibrium that respects both parties' interests can be challenging but is essential for maintaining trust and integrity in the industry.

6. Legal Expertise:

In some cases, it may be necessary to seek legal expertise, especially when navigating complex eviction procedures. Those responsible for managing properties who are not licensed property managers or who are not comfortable handling legal aspects should consider consulting an attorney to ensure that all actions taken are within the bounds of the law.

The experiences recounted in this chapter illustrate the multifaceted nature of property management and the various considerations that must be addressed when managing unauthorized occupants. By heeding the lessons learned from these experiences, those responsible for managing properties can better navigate this sensitive and challenging aspect of the industry, ultimately working toward a harmonious and equitable resolution for all parties involved.

FAQS

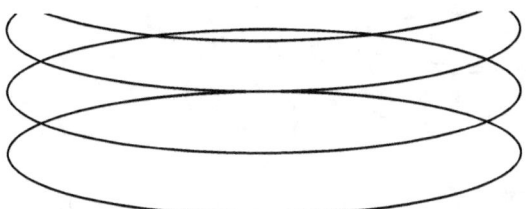

FAQ:

Frequently Asked Questions (FAQ) - Unauthorized Occupants

1. What should I do if I suspect unauthorized occupants in my property?
If you suspect unauthorized occupants, it's crucial to take proactive steps. Begin by thoroughly reviewing your lease agreements, checking for occupancy limits, and ensuring that tenants have adhered to the terms. Engage in open communication with your tenants to address any concerns or discrepancies. If needed, consult with legal professionals to explore the best course of action.

2. Can I conduct regular inspections to prevent unauthorized occupants?
Yes, conducting regular property inspections is a proactive measure to prevent unauthorized occupants. During inspections, look for signs of additional individuals residing on the property, check for safety hazards, and ensure that the number of occupants complies with the lease agreement.

3. What legal steps can I take to remove unauthorized occupants?
The legal steps to remove unauthorized occupants may vary based on your location and specific circumstances. Generally, it involves providing notice to the tenants, conducting eviction proceedings if necessary, and following legal protocols. It's highly advisable to seek legal counsel to ensure compliance with local laws and regulations.

4. Is there a way to prevent unauthorized occupants through the lease agreement?
Yes, you can take preventive measures through the lease agreement. Clearly define occupancy limits, outline the process for adding new occupants, and specify the consequences of unauthorized residency. Regularly update lease agreements to reflect any changes and communicate these terms effectively to tenants.

5. How can I foster positive relationships with tenants while addressing unauthorized occupants?
Maintaining positive relationships is key. Approach conversations about unauthorized occupants with empathy and clarity. Clearly communicate lease terms, offer solutions for compliance, and seek resolutions that are fair to both parties. Open and transparent communication is essential for fostering positive long-term relationships.

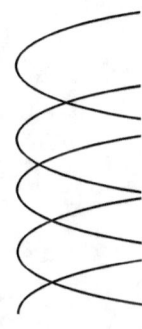

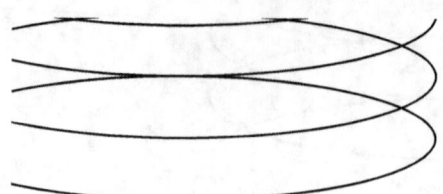

FAQ:

Frequently Asked Questions (FAQ) - Unauthorized Occupants

6. Are there community resources for property managers dealing with unauthorized occupants?
Yes, community resources such as local property manager associations, legal aid organizations, and real estate forums can provide valuable insights and support. Networking with peers in the industry allows you to share experiences and gain knowledge on effective strategies for handling unauthorized occupants.

7. What should I include in a notice to unauthorized occupants?
A notice to unauthorized occupants should include details such as the violation, the steps required for compliance, and the consequences of non-compliance. Clearly outline a timeframe for rectifying the issue and provide contact information for further communication. Ensure that the notice adheres to legal requirements in your jurisdiction.
Remember, these answers serve as general guidance, and it's advisable to consult with legal professionals to address specific situations in your property management journey effectively.

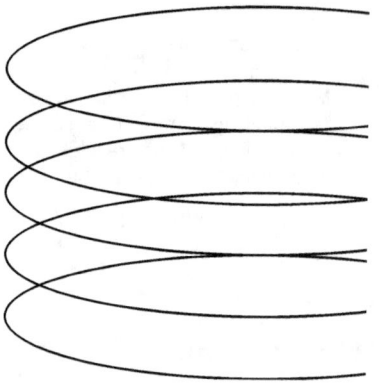

CLOSING NOTE

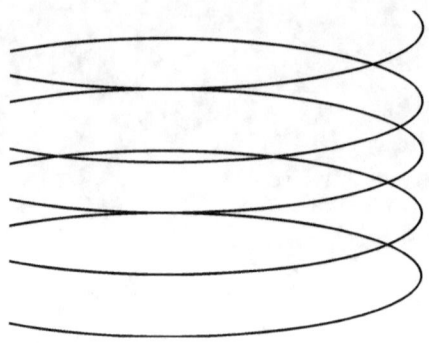

CLOSING NOTE:

As we conclude this insightful journey into the realm of unauthorized occupants and property management, we want to extend our gratitude for accompanying us through these pages. At Properly Prosper Realty LLC, we are more than just words on a page; we are dedicated professionals passionate about enhancing your property management experience.

If you find yourself in need of trusted property management services in Nevada, consider Properly Prosper Realty LLC. We are currently accepting new property management clients, and our team is ready to bring expertise and commitment to your property endeavors.

Additionally, for owners and property managers seeking advice on landlord-tenant issues, we offer 101 property management consultations. While we're not authorized legal representatives, our team consists of seasoned experts deeply rooted in the community. We are here to provide insights, strategies, and solutions tailored to your unique needs. Remember, at Properly Prosper Realty LLC, we believe in empowering property owners and managers to navigate the challenges of real estate with confidence and success. Reach out to us for a consultation, and let's embark on a journey to elevate your property management experience.

Disclaimer: Properly Prosper Realty LLC is not a law firm and does not provide legal advice. Our consultations are based on extensive industry knowledge and community expertise. For legal matters, we recommend seeking guidance from qualified legal professionals.

PROPERLYPROSPERREALTY.COM   @PROPERLYPROSPERREALTY

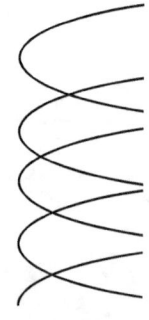

www.ingramcontent.com/pod-product-compliance
Lightning Source LLC
Chambersburg PA
CBHW062235290526
45794CB00006B/2294